CU00871995

I Beg To Differ

I Beg To Differ

Toto

Copyright © 2015 by Toto.

Library of Congress Control Number:		2020923456
ISBN:	Hardcover	978-1-6641-4435-4
	Softcover	978-1-6641-4434-7
	eBook	978-1-6641-4433-0

All rights reserved. No part of this book may be reproduced or transmitted in any form or by any means, electronic or mechanical, including photocopying, recording, or by any information storage and retrieval system, without permission in writing from the copyright owner.

Scripture quotations marked KJV are from the Holy Bible, King James Version (Authorized Version). First published in 1611. Quoted from the KJV Classic Reference Bible, Copyright © 1983 by The Zondervan Corporation.

Any people depicted in stock imagery provided by Getty Images are models, and such images are being used for illustrative purposes only.
Certain stock imagery © Getty Images.

Print information available on the last page.

Rev. date: 11/20/2020

To order additional copies of this book, contact:
Xlibris
844-714-8691
www.Xlibris.com
Orders@Xlibris.com
711851

CONTENTS

Dedicated to the ones who are, to the ones who were, and to the ones who will be

So do not fear, for I am with you; do not be dismayed, for I am your God. I will strengthen you and help you; I will uphold you with my righteous right hand.

—Isaiah 41:10

Chapter 1

They say it's the journey that counts—the lessons learned, the law of attraction, the ask and you shall receive, the attitude toward your goals, the goals you set, the having piece of mind, the positive thinking, the never quit, the give it your best shot, the receive the holy spirit, the doing things in a certain way, the believe in your dreams, the karma, the destiny, the being and thinking humble. Well, in a way, I have seen things at this moment in time. And it's not to be negative in any sort of way, but I beg to differ! I have read many books of inspiration and positive thinking. I have read poems, listened to seminars, heard many successful people say that they believe in their dreams and they come true. I would really like to know the basis—the reason—why people are really successful and why some of you and me are not. I would like to give testimony of a person, just like most of you, trying every way to make something good happen. Either it be the hard way or the easy way. The results are not that positive, but there is no giving up. Even if we try and don't succeed, there is no backing down, which, to my amazement, is a bittersweet symphony may I humbly suggest. Sometimes—no, actually most of the time—I have tried to make good things happen and they just don't seem to finish the way I want.

But there is no negative excuse for yourself (*never*). If you don't believe in yourself, no one will. So don't let no one bring you down (*ever*). And even though I have seen a lot of successful people, I ask myself, Is there a meaning? Are you born with substance of power some people possess? Or is it just the way things are meant to be? Is it a "shut your mouth and take it like a man or a woman"? Well, not me, let me tell you. Not just yet! It can't be the way; I don't want it to be. I can't be at the bottom of the pile; I was born to lead. But for some odd reason, that is the way it is. It has to be different; it just does. There should be enough for everyone, and yet in some sick joke or prank to the human race for some of you out there and me, there simply is not. Especially at a time in life where abundance is at its fullest. It's everywhere.

Here is an example of what I'm talking about. I have been through many weird journeys in this life. Once when I was eighteen years old, I got hooked up with a beautiful young girl in Mexico. At the time, I lived in Mexico because my parents sold their house in the USA, and guess what? Yes, they pulled me out of high school and it was off to Mexico. Imagine that. A journey within a journey. Well, after a couple of years in Mexico, I got hooked up with my girlfriend and decided to go to the USA to make a decent living. I was able to cross the US border, but my girl did not due to her immigration status. So we had to pay a coyote. A coyote is what they call a person who crosses people from the border of Mexico to the USA. Back then, the coyote would charge twenty dollars per person. I had to go with her for her safety. So we paid him twenty dollars on the spot, and we would pay him another twenty dollars at the end. He agreed.

It was a different experience, and imagine me at eighteen years old. I looked tall, thin with shaggy hair and the face of a baby. And my wife was as pretty as an angel. Sometimes I wonder what she saw in me. The crossing was a new and different experience and, at eighteen, a bit nerve-racking. We started out by crossing a river on a big rubber tire. It reminded me of the rubber tires we played with at lakes or at the beach when I was younger. Then we crossed some railroad tracks full of trains. As we went under some trains and over the train grips of others. I had seen on television and heard people say that the immigration officers would shoot at people, sometimes killing them with no mercy, so you could imagine a US citizen like me crossing the way of an illegal person. It was an adrenaline-rush race for safety. Just then, the thought of most of my ancestors crossed my mind. I've had many family members and friends cross the border with one thing in mind: the American dream!

The *dolares*! The making a better life for their family and themselves. Ironically, I was doing the same thing. It sent chills up my spine with many different emotions. But when you're a young kid and supposedly in love, you do the stupidest things. Wouldn't you agree? Anyway, it was done. The coyote was paid, and we all thanked God.

Chapter 2

We took a plane to sunny California, moved in with my sister, and I got a job. The future was looking good. What could possibly go wrong? *Nothing*, I thought to myself. Then all of a sudden and out of nowhere, two and a half months later, I was separated from my wife, I lost my job, and I was left thinking to myself, *What the heck happened!* It was a flash with no time to react. It was like taking candy from a baby— only in this situation, I was the baby. After that happened, I remember I went to church during the morning. It was empty, and I got on my knees and spoke to God. But he didn't answer back. I talked to him and received no answer. So I went back to Mexico defeated. And amazingly, this happened four or five times in my life. Just like that. No warning or any explanation and boom! It was done. What would you call that? 'Cause I have no answer. I am totally lost for words.

I remember one of my most magical, humble, and memorable occasions; I worked for a bottling company. I would not get paid on time. And when I would get paid, it would not be the full amount (the story of my life). I decided to talk to the owner. I asked him to liquidate what he owed me. The owner said he didn't have much money (I felt he was lying). So I told him I would take a pay cut. I just wanted my money, and I had other plans in mind. He agreed, I got paid, and that was the end of that.

At that time, I had two very important choices to make. And as you can see, I am not very good at making choices because they have not gone the way I want. I struggle on making choices even if I focus hard to make the right one. After many years, I was told it's not the choice you make that always counts; it's what you do after that will make sense to you—even if the choice was wrong or right. My first choice was to open a hamburger stand—cooking my specialty hamburgers, fries, onion rings, and maybe tacos. But I didn't have enough money to start my own hamburger stand, so I would probably have to find a partner. The second choice was to go to the snowy Rocky Mountains of Colorado and work the ski season at the hotels for three months and come back with enough money to open my own hamburger stand, buy a car, give a down payment for a real nice cozy home, and have a bit leftover for a rainy day or whatever the cause may be. At my workplace, I had some friends who had family in Colorado and who told me they would be able to help me out. And they spoke of the same story I've heard many, many times. They would speak about the snow season and what a great opportunity it was to make good money. I spoke with my family, and we agreed that doing the Rockies was the best way to go. I planned it for a couple of weeks. Curiously, word got around that I was leaving to the Rockies to work. I have a dear friend Chuy who told me his father had a friend visiting from Colorado. He said he was leaving the same day I was leaving. They spoke about me leaving to Colorado, and their friend offered to give me a ride. I met up with this guy. They called him Pepe. He seemed like a good person. We talked; we agreed and then made plans for the trip. Two days before our departure, one of my uncles wanted to tag along and work with me. So I went to Pepe and asked him if it was all right for my uncle Tonio to join us. He said it was okay, and he responded that his aunt wanted him to take her to Phoenix, Arizona. We all agreed and left two days later at 5:00 a.m.

On that day, I felt sad leaving my family. Although I gave them money to be well off, it was hurtful saying goodbye. But I had to do what I had to do. It was best for my family. I hugged them, kissed them, and then said goodbye with a couple of tears rolling down my face. I never looked back. On the other hand, I was trying to be as positive as possible. We reached the US border almost four hours later. As we were crossing the borderline, we told the immigration officer that my uncle Tonio and Pepe's aunt were going to get a permit to cross beyond El

Paso, Texas. Pepe's aunt was able to get her permit, but my uncle was unable to. He had forgotten his birth certificate at his house. Tonio asked me if I could take his bags with me and said later he would catch up to me as soon as he got his permit. I agreed, and I remember putting in the trunk two luggages and a trash bag of what seemed to be full of clothes before we said goodbye to each other. Then I went to the restroom, and as I came out, Pepe was just closing the trunk and went in his car. His aunt was also in the car, as they were both waiting for me. I saw an old man walk up next to me as I was approaching the vehicle. He said hi with a grateful smile on his face. I thought he was going to ask me for money, and as I was limited to the money I had, I shook my head at him and quickly went inside the car and told Pepe, "Let's roll." I felt a weird sensation that made me look back. And as I did, the old man was standing there nodding his head in some kind of disbelief. I felt maybe he was going to tell me something important. But him looking the way he did, I turned around; and just like that, we were on our way to Arizona then Colorado.

The desert was dry and full of Joshua trees, rocks, tumbleweeds, and a lot of orange dirt. The sky was full of gray marshmallow clouds; they looked heavy and full of snow. You could feel the cold in your bones, as it was the first week of January. Pepe had asked me to pay for half of the trip, which was food, gas, and lodge. I told him I would not pay from here to Phoenix but I would pay to Colorado. He agreed. I saw his aunt give him money for gas, and as we got hungry, we stopped for food at a nice restaurant. It was a steak house restaurant. It was delicious. As soon as we finished eating, the waiter brought the receipt for us to pay. Pepe's aunt was in the restroom, and as soon as we received the receipt, Pepe stood up and walked to the restroom himself. I felt he had no intentions of paying, so I paid. As we shivered ourselves to Arizona in the dry cold winter, we arrived at his aunt's destination. We spent the night in Phoenix, and we were off the next day early in the morning to Colorado. Pepe told me he had no money but that as soon as we hit Colorado, he would drop me off then go to his house, which was one hour away. Then he would later return and pay me. I agreed.

Chapter 3

The view from Arizona to Colorado was just awesome. Imagine, from a dry winter desert with cactus weeds on a flat piece of land everywhere you looked to an even colder winter green forest with thousands of trees lined in perfect sequence. These trees were each touching the sky at least one hundred feet up in the air. Then to the Rocky Mountains covered with a blanket of snow and even higher towering mountains. It was like God created beautiful scenery and slapped a road dab in the middle of this beautiful creation. It was a nice sight for sore eyes. What was beginning to bother me was this guy Pepe only stopped at nice expensive restaurants. He commented he never stopped at burger stands. I knew at this point he was taking advantage of me. So at that point, I was just playing it by ear. As we arrived to Denver, which was my destination, we stopped at another nice restaurant, and I remember there was a football game on. I was trying to get my thoughts straight, then Pepe interrupted and asked me if I had the keys to his car. I told him, "I don't have them. How could I? You were driving the car. Don't tell me you lost them."

"Worst," he said. "I left them in the car with the car running." He called the fire department, and they showed up and opened his door. The firefighters asked who was the person who left the keys inside. I couldn't believe what happened next. This guy Pepe pointed at me. The firefighters looked at me and just shook their heads. I told them it was not me, but I don't think they believed me. I looked at Pepe and told him, "Very funny" in a sarcastic way. After that incident, we were on our way. It took us a while to find the address of my friend's family members, but we did manage to find it. I told Pepe, "So will you be back with half of the money I spent?"

He said, "Yeah, I'll be back. Don't worry."

And when most people say don't worry, I worry, because to me that means "screw you." So I asked, "Are you sure?"

He said, "Come on. I know Chuy's dad real good.

I told him, "Well, pop the trunk open so I can get my bags out." So I took out two luggage bags and a trash bag full of clothes. I set it on the ground. I told Pepe, "Can you wait for me while I see if the people are home?

He said, "Yeah, don't worry." (There goes that saying again.) "I'll wait. You go ahead."

I shivered my way to the door. It was as cold as an icebox in Denver, and not knowing what to expect and not much money at hand, I suddenly felt something special. I got the courage like a Mexican warrior on the edge of a cliff and no place to go. He would not surrender. He would wrap his flag around his body and jump. So I jumped. I knocked on the door. As it began to open, there was a young man close to my age. He said, "How can I help you?" I told him I was Sergio's friend from Chihuahua. He said, "Give me one second." As I stood there, I had many mixed emotions (many of them). An older man came out to greet me. He asked if I was Al.

I answered, "Yes, sir. Are you Alejandro?"

He responded, "Yes, I am."

"So Sergio called you?" I replied.

He said, "Of course, I thought you would be here a couple of days ago." Then he added, "Did you come alone?"

"Of course not," I told him. "I came with a friend."

He said, "You must have good friends, but are they invisible?"

"Invisible!" I said. Then as I turned to the street, the car—along with Pepe—had disappeared. My luggage was there on the ground. I responded in the only way I could, and that was, "Damn!" Everything got quiet around me, and the only thing I felt and heard was a cool breeze with a silent but loud whisper say, "Sucker!" The whole city was filled of stony gray clouds, and the streets were filled of white crushed snow. I told the old man, "He just dropped me off and left just like that."

The old man said, "By the way, did I tell you my name is Alejandro?"

"Yes, you did," I responded.

As I walked in, he introduced me to his wife, daughter, son, and a friend, who was a heavyset man. The heavyset man offered me a drink of brandy and coke. He had a white collar on and looked like a priest. I did not want to be a bother, so I declined the drink. He said, "Amigo, you will take this drink with me" in a please-drink-with-me kind of way. So I agreed, and it was bottoms up. Alejandro asked me what I was thinking of doing. I told him I wanted to go to Breckenridge and work in the hotels for the snow season. He said it was a good-paying job for the snow season and added there were hundreds of skiers up there. I felt a bit relieved, and with a drink I had taken, I felt pretty confident. We hit it off from the start. I felt really welcomed (it's a good thing my neighbors at work had phoned them that I was going there). It totally changed the atmosphere. Later on that evening, I found out the heavyset man was a Catholic priest. He looked very intelligent and educated. I believe his name was George—a very outgoing and real nice person, probably a bit on the brandy side but nevertheless a cool person. Alejandro told me he had a small business selling carpets at a flea market during the weekends and installing them during the week. He had the help of a two-man crew. Everybody there was super nice. We spoke about Mexico, California, then Colorado. By the way, their regular tap water in Denver, Colorado, tasted crisp and clean and came out cold. It tasted fresher and better than the bottled water we purchased at the store. It was amazing. Well, anyway, after a while, the priest had to call it a night because he had a mass to give early next morning. So I shook his hand and told him it was a pleasure to meet him. He told me I was a good kid and left with his blessings. Alejandro told me I could sleep in the basement. I had never been in a basement before. I had only seen the ones I saw in movies, and they were kind of creepy. So I followed him to the basement, and it was a normal room with two beds and a dresser in it. One of his helpers was in one bed, and the other was empty. They called him Shorty due to his height, of course. He was quiet and not much of a talker. I felt funny with my two luggages and a trash bag full of clothes. I looked like a hiker going up the Himalayas. I looked weird. I settled in, then we called it a night.

I awoke the next morning and was able to shower and get myself ready for the Rockies. The family was nice enough to offer me breakfast. We had—guess what? A Denver omelet with beans and fried ham on the side. It was good. Alejandro offered to take me to the airport. I told him, "No, it's okay. I'll be taking the bus. The airplane is too expensive."

He laughed and said, "Not for the airplane. They have the buses that go to Breckenridge in front of the airport."

I felt like an idiot and said, "Of course." Then I added, "Yes, I will accept the ride. Thank you!" So off we went. I saw a good part of the city of Denver on the way to the airport. I think the old man took me the long way to show off his city, which was nice. I saw Mile High Stadium, the Nuggets and Avalanche arena, the underway construction of Coors Field, and John Elway's number 7 Toyota dealer. It was different and really cool. Once we hit the airport, I went in as Alejandro waited for me in his van and bought my ticket. It was a purchase for a one-way pass from Denver to Breckenridge. I was super positive, energetic, and full of dreams. I was feeling blessed. Maybe George the priest's blessing had worked. No! Wait a minute, it did work! I was sure of it. I was on my way to conquering the Rocky Mountains. I felt it in my hands. I thought to myself, *One big step for me, one giant step for my family.* The ticket was eighty-five dollars, and I only had $180. I did not panic one bit. Failure was not an option. I would get a job, save money, and not worry much. By the way, I was going to have free room and board and good pay. I was on cloud nine. So after I purchased the ticket with a smile on my face so big that if I had ChapStick on my lips, my smile was so big I would stain my ears with it, I went to Alejandro and told him how thankful I was for his and his family's helping hand and kindness. Then I gave Alejandro twenty dollars for the ride. At first he didn't want to accept it. Alejandro said, "Thank you, but I think you need it more." I told him, "It's not much, but the least you can do is take it." He didn't respond, so I slipped it in his shirt pocket. He gave me his phone number and asked if I would drop by on my way back. I thanked him again and told him I would stop by on my way back and thank him again. He said we'd have some brandy; I agreed. He left on his way, and I was on my way to one of the most beautiful places on earth during the snow season.

Chapter 4

I remembered friends who had been there talk about how nice it was. They talked about beautiful ice sculptures, amazing log cabin mansions, and wonderful people. I also remembered them talking about working two jobs—one at a hotel and the other at a bar or restaurant, making money and saving it. They would not spend much at all because the food and board was free. And there was no reason for leaving the resort to spend money. They had it made. My family would be proud of me. I knew I was; after all, what could possibly go wrong? Absolutely nothing, right? And yes, I had two luggages and a trash bag full of clothes. Pathetic, yes; worried, no. The speaker sounded off, and it sounded loud and clear. It said, "Everybody going to Breckenridge, please have your ticket at hand and form a line outside the blue line next to the van number (I don't remember the number). Anyway, as I boarded the van, there were five Chinese tourists taking a hundred pictures a minute. There were also an older couple, two older ladies, and me, of course. We headed off to the Rockies, and besides the view I had seen from Phoenix to Denver and every time I had been to Dodger Stadium, the road from Denver to Breckenridge was so beautiful that I would say it was heavenly. I saw wonderful mountains covered with rock-hard ice with see-through blue waterfalls. I saw a huge frozen lake. And at one point, I saw two trucks on top of the frozen lake and people fishing on top of that same lake. It was as sturdy as the ground we walked on. I also saw a herd of buffalo running under the highway to come through the other side. I guess besides being on a horse, this was the closest you could get to a buffalo on the run without being in any kind of danger. It was powerful!

The higher we got, the more beautiful it seemed. I saw houses out yonder (far away). (This whole scenario makes me talk like countryfolk). I thought to myself, *Wow, those people living in those huge beautiful houses are living it up while living. Those people and I are very blessed.* I was taking all this in when out of nowhere, my thoughts of my family just hit me hard as if they were consuming the view I was watching or experiencing my emotions. I wished them well mentally, and I had a tear drop down my eye. It was a tear of joy, sadness, and prosperity. This tear was more beautiful than any snowflake or diamond I had ever seen. It was a true tear. At that moment, I said to myself, *I wish my family were here with me so they could enjoy these wonderful views. Really, I do.* As we got to Breckenridge, it was an ice-cold but sunny day. I saw some ice sculptures like the ones you see at weddings or fancy parties. The only difference was that these sculptures were huge—I mean, super huge. I also saw beautiful log cabins that were big like mansions. We passed through downtown Breckenridge. It was a real nice and cozy street with nice little shops on each side. The town looked like those little model toy towns you see at toy stores. Funny and strange, I might add. For some awkward reason, I felt like Lloyd and Harry (you know, the guys from *Dumb and Dumber* as they're arriving to aspen). We stopped at a real nice hotel. I can't remember the name, but if I go there again, I can tell you exactly which one it was. On my way off the bus, I asked the driver if he knew where the employment recruiting facility was. He told me he would take me there as soon as he finished unloading the van. And at no extra cost, I might add. He said he thought I was cool. He also said I reminded him of his older boy—Joshua, I believe he said. I thought that was cool. I started helping the driver unload so he could finish faster. I was blocks away from my new employment, and it felt as good as winning a little league baseball game when I was younger.

Thinking of that job and thinking good thoughts of my family kept me stable, and I would not get that homesick feeling. And just like that, we were off to the beginning of a good future for my family and I. I thanked the driver when he dropped me off. He wished me good luck and left. I got my ridiculous but unique baggage and headed to the front office. A bit tired but then again relieved, I opened the door to human resources and felt like if I was walking into fame. There must had been fifteen to twenty people working in that office. I just said to myself, *Ka-ching.* I walked up to the secretary at the front desk and asked, "How are you doing?" She looked at me and looked confused. *It has to be my luggage,* I thought.

She answered, "I'm okay. How are you?"

"I'm a bit cold, but I can manage," I answered in a cocky but friendly way.

She asked, "How can I help you?" I told her I was ready to work and came for a job at the hotel. She said, "For next summer?"

I said, "No, for now." She paused and asked me where I was coming from. I told her, "Denver—well, actually, Mexico, but I am a US citizen, and I am ready to work." She said, "Give me a minute" and walked off to another office. I was getting impatient. As she came back out, she told me to go to the office next door and go to division 1 and see what they could do for me. "What do you mean?" I replied.

She told me, "There are no openings whatsoever until the next snow season, but you can go next door and apply for this spring. Maybe they're still hiring." My goodness! My jaw dropped to the ground faster and harder than any cartoon character had ever dropped a jaw. I only had seventy-five dollars and change to my name. I couldn't think or react. My face turned as pale as the outside winter snow. The lady asked if I was all right. "Hello?" she said in a high-pitched voice. The second time she asked, I did respond. I told her there must be some kind of mistake. "No, we hire in November and December for the snow season. And I am sorry to say, but every position has been filled," she said.

I thought to myself that the money I had would not get me far. My mind was boggled. I had to ask her again, "Excuse me, ma'am. So there are no openings at all—nowhere?" She replied she was sorry, and she looked really sorry. She said I came two weeks too late. I told her, "Well, thank you, and I apologize for any inconvenience I have caused." She told me not to worry and wished me luck. I felt like telling her I needed a job, not luck. But I did not say a word. I walked out of the office with two luggages and a trash bag full of clothes. I was really deeply lost for a moment. You know, sometimes the most simple task seems unreachable until you clear your mind and rethink or reprogram your brain. I regained thinking notion after a couple of deep breaths and thought to myself that if I'd go directly to the hotel, they would probably hire me. Not remembering all the hiring was done by the office, I had just left. I asked a young couple if they would tell me how to get to the hotel. They told me the shuttle would take me directly to the hotel, and there was a shuttle stop around the corner. So I walked to the shuttle stop, and there was one coming every ten minutes or so. The stops were full of people with big smiles on their faces, skis and ski boards in their hands. As the shuttle stopped, it had big racks so skiers could put their equipment or, as they would call them, toys. I mounted the shuttle, and I felt people staring at me, not really saying a word but oddly looking. I was spiritually crushed. And to put the icing on the cake, I was among people who were in good standing and I was at the same place at the same time as them. Everybody seemed to be having a good time while I was in an opposite scenario. I felt like the only rotten apple in the orchard of paradise. None of their positiveness or good humor or luck for that matter rubbed off on me. Why! Is that not weird when other people tell you what they believe and it goes their way? We were all there together. It was something so out of balance. So I repeated a couple of times to myself, *I got one more shot left. Let's see what happens.*

Chapter 5

I motivated myself by saying, "If these people could do it, why not me?" Yeah! Why not me? After minutes of saying that, I was positive and back on the right track again with only seventy-five dollars and some change in my pocket. As soon as we arrived to the hotel, I took a deep breath, got off the shuttle, and headed straight to the front office and asked for a job. And as if the world was against me, guess what happened? I was denied. So after everything changed, my game plan had to change also. So my next move was to get shelter for the night and fast. I asked the front desk what the cheapest room in the hotel was running for. When I was told the price, I almost fainted. I asked how much a regular food plate was. When I was told the price, I almost fainted a second time. A good thing was that the coffee in the lobby was free. So then I served my coffee and purchased cookies from a vending machine they had across the hall. Good thing because I was starving. Hmm, I had purchased the best Oreo cookies ever! Plus the case of me not eating anything all day had something to do with that.

Just then, I was hit by a forgotten memory—like an uncontrollable force of a memory. It was a similar situation. One in San Diego with my wife, my daughter, and my three-month-old son. We were stranded in Downtown San Diego with ten dollars at hand and no place to go. We had just come back from Mexico. My family members did not want to help us out at that time. I was a mess in tears. I remember I bought cookies, milk, and water. It lasted almost all day. We were in front of a tall building just thinking of what to do. After hours of phone use and seeing what was going to happen, a security guard (God bless his soul) securing the building we were in front of saw us, and he probably knew or felt what was going on. He came up to us and let us in for more water and a place to sit and let us use the restrooms and phone. As he let us in, I heard him say to himself in a whispering way, "I hope I don't get fired for this." Isn't that amazing sometimes that a person who does not know you at all will help you out more than one who does? Or more than a family member for that reason. I offered him cookies. He smiled in gratitude and replied, "No, thank you." Then I went on calling for support. Finally, a family member agreed to pick us up later on that night. It was one of my aunts, and I was grateful. The only thing that bothered me a bit was when my aunt arrived to pick us up, she went with one condition: that we join her religion. She said it was the right one. I never did join her religion. She, on the other hand, is now out of it. I guess we don't always do what we preach.

So check this out. I'm in the lobby back at the hotel thinking to myself, *What am I going to do?* And let me tell you, honestly, I was thinking of robbing someone and going back home—just stop with all the letdowns and just do it. I had the same thought in San Diego. I took a deep breath in both situations and kept on thinking and talking to God. I asked why. Why! But no answer. I had finished my coffee and cookies, and still, nothing clicked. I felt like I was racing against time. Soon enough, the hotel host walked up to me and said, "Can I help you?" I told him I had no place to go at the moment with my face turning red of embarrassment, but I was nevertheless energetic—well, if you could call it that in my desperate situation. "I am looking for a job," I told him.

He said, "I cannot help you, and you have to leave. *Now.*"

"But I have no place to go. Plus it's dark and freezing outside."

"You need to go."

"You can't kick me out. I'll freeze to death."

"Well, call the police station," he grumbled. So I did. I explained to them my situation and asked if I could spend the night at their station. They told me I had to be a criminal to sleep there. I said, "Damn!" and hung up. I thought to myself, *To serve and protect huh!* The host walked up to me again and said I had to leave immediately. I asked him to give me a couple of minutes and if I could serve myself another cup of coffee. He replied with a disrespectful and angry tone, "No! You may not." Just then, I remembered Alejandro, the old man. He had given me his number. So I asked the front desk if I could use their phone. They said no, and I told them I was going to call a friend in Denver who would help me out. They agreed and said, "Just one call, and that's it."

As I was dialing Alejandro's number, I was desperately needing help, and I was hoping he would pick up. The phone rang, and Alejandro answered. I explained what had happened. He chuckled and said to me, "I was thinking it was too late in the snow season for hire." I totally agreed. He said, "So what can I do for you?"

I told him, "I was just wondering if you could do me a big favor by wiring me just enough money to get a van ride back to Denver. I have no money, but I can pay you back with work."

"How much is the ticket?" he said.

I asked for the price, and a manager walked up to me and said $215. "Damn," I said. "Why so much?"

"This is a special trip," he answered.

"There is nothing special about me, and if there were, I would either be here working or on vacation." I told Alejandro the price, and he said with no hesitation, "Here is my card number. Charge the amount needed." Just like that. I was surprised but very grateful and thankful. Once the card was accepted, they had to treat me like a guest. I saw a change in the face of the host and asked him for a cup of coffee. The manager who did help me out said in a vengeful voice to the host, "Make it two cups. I'll take one cream and two sugars. And how would you like yours?

I replied, "I would like two cream, three sugars, and a drop of honey." He left and came back with our coffee and an I-can't-believe-this look on his face. I got along real good with the manager. He gave me his business card and offered me work for the next snow season with a full-time job and a three-month pay. I thanked him. Is it not amazing the way some people act in a negative or positive way for no particular reason? Do we trigger that attitude, or does it come from a negative or positive vibe? Are some of us just naturally mean and others nice? The funny part is none of this attitude has to do with rich or poor. Does it? I am starting to think that none of us make it on our own. We all need a strong backbone—whether it be the leader of a nation, a high school teacher, a sports coach, a mother, a father, or a friend.

After a couple of hours, a van came zooming in the half-moon driveway. The driver honked two times and stepped out of the company van. Out popped an older man with a reddish face, his hair the color of white onions. He had a grumpy but spiffy look. Out of nowhere, he seemed to have a kick to his energetic, tired, old look. He then shouted my name in a high loud voice. I shouted back, "Here I am!"

He said, "There's no need to shout, boy" while he smiled and winked. I smiled back. He picked up my ticket from the front office. He then turned around and shouted, "All aboard. Let's get out of this altitude." Then he looked at my luggage and remarked, "What kind of baggage is this?"

I replied, "It's two luggages and a bag of clothes, and yes, it's mine."

Then he asked, "What kind of tourist are you?"

I did not want to explain or go into detail of my unsatisfactory journey, but on the other hand, I did not want to disrespect the old man. So I told him a little white lie. I told him I had served my time in the navy and I was just traveling looking for some action. We boarded the van, and about ten minutes later, he asked, "Did you find it?"

"Did I find what?" I told him.

"The action," he said.

"Oh! Yeah, yeah, a little bit here, a little bit there. You know how it is." And to my surprise, this man had also served in the navy. Then he asked my rank and what station and division I was from or something like that. And let me tell you, I have respect for every troop serving, but I have no idea how they operate. I looked at him, and I was pretty sure he wanted to talk all night. "I served on the SS Minnow," I told him.

"I've never heard of it," he said.

I told him, "You must have." And deep inside, I felt like a doofus. With a smile on my face and a murmur, I said, "Haven't you seen *Gilligan's Island*?"

He replied, "What did you say?" I quickly changed the subject to what a great scenery the road we were taking was during the daytime. And that set him off a couple of hours on a history course, which I enjoyed. There was one thing about this old man: he was racist, especially toward Mexicans. But he was old and brought up the old way, and at that time, there was change in the air. Once we arrived at Alejandro's house in Denver, I got off and told the van driver to give me a minute. He had got off and opened the back door of his van. I went to the front door of the house. I felt the same way I had felt when I first arrived and just a bit more embarrassed this time. I knocked on the door, and guess who was there? The priest, Alejandro, and his family. "Welcome back," Alejandro said to me. I turned to the van on the street, and yes, it was gone. The only thing on the street was snow and two luggage bags and a trash bag full of clothes. *Here we go again*, I thought to myself. As I went in the house, they all cracked a couple of jokes on my behalf. I smiled; they laughed. It was cool. The priest offered me a drink. I took it with no hesitation.

He told me, "Ah! You're a quick learner." I smiled.

Alejandro then asked me, "So what's next?"

I told him, "Let's get to work if it's okay with you." He asked if I was ready. I had an intense ready-to-kick-butt look on my face. Then I replied, "I was born ready!" He had an oh-my-goodness look on his face.

Chapter 6

Alejandro was a nice man to help me out like that. He told me to take the next day off so I could get some rest and be ready for the day after. I disagreed and told him I was ready to go, but that was the way he wanted it. So I agreed. Later on that night, he led me to the basement. I saw his worker Shorty there, and I greeted him, and he greeted me back. I put my luggage away. It felt cold as only a basement could feel so cold. So I covered up and called it a night.

The next morning, I got up, got dressed, and was ready to go. I went outside and helped Alejandro and his workers load the van with carpets and tools. When we were done, Alejandro asked me if I knew how to cook. I told him I did. He said, "Well, then go cook yourself breakfast and get ready for tomorrow." So I went inside and started cooking. I was thinking of my family and was hoping they were still all right with the money I left them. The next day, I started working for Alejandro, and I was doing the best I could. The days passed, and on the weekend, they took me to the flea market to help with carpet sales. I was good at selling. I was selling carpets left and right and making appointments for installations. Alejandro's workers were not too happy with that. But they did not speak a word of English, and at that time, mostly everybody spoke English, so they would take me. Soon Alejandro would lend me his car. He would say I was a smart kid and would encourage me to make a living in Denver and would tell me he would help me. "I know you will make it here," he would say. I would tell him I just wanted to make enough money to be with my family, run a business, and have a nice place to stay. He replied, "Well, I'm here to help you." I thanked him.

I quickly learned how to install carpets. I would install carpets in the morning during the week and sell carpets during the weekend. Since I had permission to drive Alejandro's car, I got a part-time job in telemarketing in the afternoon. I was saving my money and just waiting for winter to be over, then it was off to my precious ones. All was going smooth; nothing else could possibly go wrong.

One day, Alejandro was thinking of knocking down an old tree in his yard. He had thought of knocking down that old tree for a couple of years. It just got bigger and bigger. I asked him, "What's holding you back, old man?"

He replied, "It's too expensive to pay somebody, Mr. Youth."

I answered, "Well, that I am, and I could probably cut it down for you." He asked if I knew how to cut down trees. I told him, "Let's find out." It took me a day and a half to chop it down, and boy, was it a mission. It was a good thing that the sun came out for those couple of days. But I came, I cut, and I cleaned everything. When I was done, I was a mess. Just imagine me with thorns all over my torn clothes and scratches all over. I looked like I had fought with a tiger in the middle of a jungle, and believe me, I did. Nevertheless, I took it down limb from limb. It was no match for my resistance or my chainsaw. Well, the chainsaw was not mine; Alejandro rented it. But for that day and a half, it was in my hand. It was mine. I was the dominator. Alejandro was amazed and grateful. "I am proud of you," he said.

I told him, "So am I."

He then asked in a playful, sarcastic way, "Do you know anything about roofing?"

I told him, "No, but I can learn."

"Just as I thought," he said. "You were up in that tree for so long that the leaves went in your brain." We both laughed. That day, he gave me some extra money and told me to take a shower, relax, and go with the guys for some beers. So I did. We went out for a couple hours.

As it was time for me to leave, I told the guys I was taking off and asked them if they wanted to leave. One guy seemed mad; they called him Gordo. He said in an angry tone of voice, "Now that old Alejandro is not here. You're nobody, so sit down and shut up." I knew he was upset because Alejandro and I were real good friends. I did not appreciate the way he shouted at me. I told him, "Look, I don't want any problems." (Deep inside, I did feel like making a problem, but he was not worth it.) I was just tired, and I wanted to go rest.

Then Shorty jumped in on our conversation and said, "There is no problem here. Just stay with us a bit longer, and we will all leave together." I agreed because I did not want them all against me. Half an hour passed, and they were still there, and it looked like they had no intention to leave. I got up and left. As I was leaving, Shorty caught up to me and asked where I was going. I told him, "To sleep." He said, "Come on. Let's stay a little while longer." I disagreed, then he agreed to leave, and we both took off. I could sense he planned or was planning something against me—just by the look on his face. I didn't say anything because I could have been wrong. We got to the house. I put the keys on the key hanger in the kitchen and called it a night.

Early the next morning, Alejandro came rushing down the stairs like a quarter horse at the Kentucky Derby. I mean, faster than a lightning bolt. He looked furious. He walked up to me, and at that moment, I turned to Shorty's bed, and it was empty. I don't know why, but I had imagined what was going to happen next. I got up and left. As I was leaving Shorty caught up to me and asked where I was going. I told him to sleep. He said, come on let's stay a little while longer. I disagreed, then he agreed to leave and we both took off. I could sense he planned or was planning something against me. Just by the look on his face. I didn't say anything, because I could have been wrong. We got to the house, I put the keys on the key hanger in the kitchen and called it a night. Early the next morning Alejandro came rushing down the stairs like a quarter horse at the Kentucky derby. I mean faster than a lightning bolt. He looked upset. He walked up to me, and at that moment I turned to Shorty's bed and it was empty. I don't know why, but I had bad feeling on what was going to happen next. Alejandro raised his voice at me, saying, "What happened last night?"

I told him, "What happened with what?"

"My car is missing. I trust you and this is how you repay me."

I told him, "Wait a minute, there is no reason for you to be upset."

"I don't care what you say. Tell me what happened to my car."

I told him, "Me and Shorty came in early. I left the keys on the key hanger, came to the basement, and went to sleep. And that was it."

He said, "Nonsense."

I told him, "What do you mean?" (I felt real sad at that moment.)

"Don't lie to me," he said. I hollered back to him and told him that I was not lying. "Yes, you are," he said in a very awkward way. As we were arguing, guess who showed up walking down the stairs like he had no worries in the world? It was Shorty with a no-sleep look on his face. He had his shirt tucked out, and he was tumbling down the basement with a big smile and the car keys at hand. I said to myself, *Aha! Shorty took the car.*

"What happened!" Alejandro asked Shorty.

Shorty told him in a calm, cynical way, "I took the car and went back to drink some more, why? What happened?

I thought I was in the clear, when Alejandro exploded, blew his top off, and said, "You cannot disrespect me, none of you. It's for the best if both of you leave." My eyes were wide open in disbelief. I thought to myself, *Not again. So close yet so far like always.* But I took a deep breath, got my stuff together without arguing or asking for any explanation, and left just like that. Shorty followed behind me. I told him, "See what you caused?" He apologized. "Now what?" I told him. "I didn't charge Alejandro what he owes me (I was too stupid and too proud to see him at all), and now I don't have a place to go." He told me he had a place to stay, but I could not stay there. I wished him good luck and told him I was leaving. He asked where. I told him, "Home. I am going home." He then mentioned he had a friend in Dalhart, Texas, near Amarillo, who was always hiring people for his gardening business. He said he would call him and there would be no problem for me getting a job. What was I thinking? There are no gardens to be serviced in the winter. But I guess at that moment in time, I just wanted to work and fulfill my only objective, and I was on a mission (and I wasn't thinking straight).

We went to a park to think things through. A warm sun came out as if to cover my coldness. There we were sitting near a frozen bench. I was glancing up and thinking to myself, *I wonder how my family is doing. I hope they are okay.* I took a second glance, and I thought, *Indeed, the sun does shine for everybody! The rich, poor, sad, happy and for people in good times or bad times. It shines the same for everyone—no discrimination, no questions asked. That is a beautiful thing.* Just then, I felt some inspiration. I said to myself, *We are all together in this magical, wonderful world. And we don't give up.* I took a deep breath and asked Shorty for his friend's address in Texas and said, "Let's roll."

I was on my way to the bus station. Before we could leave the park, I saw Alejandro's son-in-law driving around the park. He stopped next to us and asked us how we were doing. I told him we were fine and asked for a ride to the bus station. He asked us, "What happened to you guys?" Shorty explained what happened and asked him if he could take me to the bus station and told him he'd explain later. Deep inside, I think old man Alejandro told his son-in-law to look for us. I think Shorty went back to work for him. I could just feel it. I never thanked Alejandro, but I did wish God would bless him. He really did help me out. We got to the bus station in Denver, and well, I did take a bus to Dalhart, Texas. And you never know, maybe this was the best way. Have you ever heard of that saying "Three strikes and you're out"? Well, I had two strikes and a foul tip, so I was still hanging in there.

Chapter 7

I arrived to my destination at around 5:00 a.m. There were no taxicabs in that small town. It was really small. There was snow on the ground, and on the rooftops, I saw icicles on the edge of every roof. The town was as quiet as a student taking a final exam in the library. I could even hear myself thinking. The bus station was just opening. Actually, it was just a small office with a bench in the front. I asked the old lady who was opening the office if she was familiar with the name or address I had. She must had been at least eighty years old. Suprisingly, she did know where they lived and gave me directions. It was not very far, maybe six to eight blocks. So I picked up my two luggages and the trash bag full of clothes and was on my way. My toes were getting numb, my fingers were losing feeling, and I could not even feel my nose. It was freezing. It was a good thing I did not have to walk too far.

As I went up to the house, the sun was not up yet. But I did see lights on in the house, and I saw some movement inside. And stupid me did not get their phone number off Shorty. I was thinking, *What on earth am I doing here? I should have gone back home.* I was getting discouraged, but I had to do it. So I did. *Here we go one more time.* I knocked on the door. A man in his late forties or early fifties opened the door and asked me, "How can I help you?" He looked at my bags and was in a curious mode. I presented myself and told him what I was there for. He scratched his head and told me, "Son, winter is not over yet, and it won't be for a month or so. I have no work for you." I said to myself, *Just as I thought. Damn.* But then he exclaimed, "Give me a second! Let me see if I can help you." He went inside his house, disappearing in an instant then reappearing in another. He walked me out to a real nice Jeep Wrangler. He said, "Put your stuff in the back and get in the front and get some sleep. You should be fine. It will get warmer in a matter of no time as soon as the sun comes up." And a weird fact is that it is colder in the winter from sunup to maybe 2:00 a.m. And for about a couple of hours, it's just not cold; and before the sun comes out, it gets to super freezing temperatures. Isn't that weird? Well, I think it is. I went inside the Jeep. I thought the man was cool. His name was Carlos. The sun was peeking through the small town of Dalhart. About an hour later, Carlos brought me a cup of steaming good-smelling coffee with a piece of sweet bread. I was thankful. I asked, "So did Shorty call you?"

He said, "No, he didn't."

I told him, "My goodness, I thank you for helping me out."

He said, "I never open my door to strangers, but you look different."

I told him, "Different how?"

He said, "Just different."

I told him, "That makes me lucky, right?" He smiled and went back inside. Later on that day, I found out he had fired Shorty. I was flabbergasted. He then told me he had no job for me but his son did. His son was the town house, business, and farm painter and was really good. He told me he needed assistance. "I would be glad to work for him," I said.

He then said, "Good. Just make yourself comfortable, and he will be out in a couple hours." I thanked him again, then he turned and went back inside his cozy house. And I could bet it was nice and warm too. I was trying to be as positive as possible. I was saying to myself over and over, "This is going to be a good day. This is going to be a good day." I rested my head back and closed my eyes, and I was ready for work. Carlos's son came out later on. He must had been a bit older than me. He presented himself as Carl, but deep inside, I knew his name was as his father's, Carlos. He looked a bit of an uptight person. He explained to me the job description and the pay. I agreed. We headed off to a big place out in the country. You could see the lot on that farm for miles. It was huge. Just from the entrance to the property at the edge of the highway to the house itself was about a quarter mile. The whole farm was covered with snow. It was a wonderful view. As we arrived to our job destination, we unloaded the tools and went inside and started working. It seemed like we had worked together for years. We hit it off from the start. I was feeling good working and learning from a paint specialist.

At the end of the day, he liked the way I worked, so he raised my pay, and I was happy. He asked me if I had enough money for a motel. I told him I did but not for many days. He suggested I stay at the home out in the country, the one we were painting. It was empty out in the country with nothing in sight, and the owners would not move in until the remodeling was complete. I agreed, and that was that. In the daytime, it looked like an empty house being remodeled—no flooring with walls and roof needing fixing. There was an old pool table in the middle of one of the living rooms with a couple of pool balls and a broken pool stick to accompany it. It was a real nice fixer-upper. But at nighttime, with the lights off, you could put your hands in front of your face and you could not see it. It was dark, and I mean creepy dark. I slept in the basement because I thought it would be safer there. The only bad thing was that it was darker in there. I don't know why, but at night, all the scary movies I had ever seen in the past would pop into my mind. So imagine, I felt, heard, and saw those scary things there. And when it's dark and you're alone, you think something is going to happen even if there is nothing there. You see your darkest fears in the darkness. So what I would do was pray myself to sleep. The most annoying part, I remember, were the coyotes—especially the first couple of days. They would scratch at the front door for the longest time. It was a bit frightening at first, but I endured. What really worried me was if we had left a window or a door open or if they would break in. But nevertheless, I was cautious (scared silly!). And I was not about to go check. And let me tell you something very uplifting: even after the darkest night, sunlight follows. And thank God, it did.

After days went by, I met Carl's whole family. They were real nice people. Carl invited me to watch the Super Bowl at his sister and brother-in-law's house. I accepted the invitation and had a good time there. Although my team was not in it, it was a classic. Everything was good. I also remember one day, Carl had sent me into town for some paint supplies that we were low on. He lent me his jeep. As I got into the city, I got to the paint store, hopped off the jeep, and bought some paint rolls and brushes. On my way outside the store, I saw a yard sale across the street; and in that yard sale, I saw a box that said "music." So I went to go check it out. They had nothing but mostly country music cassettes, except for a U2 *War* cassette. I purchased it for a dollar. I went back to the Jeep and popped it in and headed back to work. There is a saying that makes me laugh when I hear it—especially when it's against me, but nevertheless true. They say to stir up some fame, go to sleep. The next day, you will be famous or talked about. So any of you people in the stardom field out there, do this if you want attention and you will not be disappointed. Well, anyway, the next day, as Carl came in the house, I was already up and working. I said hi to him, and he replied hi but in a slumpy, upset kind of way. He was quiet for half a day, then at lunchtime, he said he wanted to talk to me. I told him, "Are you okay?"

He then asked me in a serious tone of voice, "Why were you speeding and listening to my radio full blast yesterday?" At that moment, I did not know what to say. He came out of nowhere with that accusation. So this came out of my mouth: "Are you kidding me, Carl?"

He said, "Well, maybe not speeding, but you were listening to the radio full blast."

I told him, "I bought a U2 cassette, and I was listening to it, but not full blast. I apologize for any inconvenience."

He said, "I should've known. Hey, don't worry. It's not your fault. It's the people of this town who are pretty off. They told my dad yesterday that someone else was in my Jeep listening to loud crazy music."

I told him, "That's weird."

Carl responded by saying, "No, you don't understand."

I told him, "Understand what?"

He said, "This town believes rock is the devil's music." I was speechless. He said, "Really, there are no rock and roll radio stations, no MTV, no rock period." I felt like I was in that movie *Footloose*, only I was not gonna make a big scene about it. It was weird. Later on that night, I explained to Carl my view on music while listening to—guess what? Rock music. And we had a six pack of beer. We came to a mutual agreement on the topic. It was cool.

As the days past, I was working twelve to fourteen hours a day. It was all good. We even finished three weeks ahead of schedule. Carl invited me and his dad to lunch one day. I remember I had some fish and chips. Either I was very hungry or they were good cooks at that restaurant shack, because the fish was tasty. Carl's dad, Carlos, was telling me there was a good future here in Dalhart to raise a nice decent family. I was listening to what they were saying and had some thoughts about it. But I had a goal set in my mind, and that was to go back to my family and get a business going. But I kept it to myself, and everything was good. After finishing our job, we immediately received another big job with good pay. Carl and I were happy. Carl bragged about him and I being a strong team. I agreed by saying, "Not just strong but powerful." And with almost a month remaining for the snow season to end, I was excited.

Chapter 8

Then it was time for me to get paid. And remember how at the beginning I told you I would not get paid in full or on time, then I remarked that's the story of my life? Well, it happened again. As we were doing numbers, Carl told me straight-out, "You know I am not going to be able to pay you in full. I can't pay you that much."

I asked him, "What do you mean?"

He said, "It's too much."

I told him, "But that is what I worked for. Plus we finished ahead of time, and you received an extra bonus."

He said, "Yes, but come on. Give me a break."

I told him, "You give me a break. You got paid in full, so I don't understand why I can't."

"I just can't," he said.

I just put my head down and took a deep breath. I was sick and tired and very, very upset. I understood him having to pay his bills, and I didn't have the heart to get mad at him. *Now what?* I thought to myself. After everything I had gone through and the little money I had to show for it, I said that was it. I decided to go home to my family. Home is where the heart is, and my family is in my heart. I thanked Carl and Carlos and told them I was leaving. Carl said in an apologetic way, "We still have that big job to do. I would like your help." If he had paid me in full, I would have roughed it out with him; after all, he was a nice guy. But no money, no honey. Both of them asked me to return. I did not want to argue my case because I was still upset. But on the other hand, I was still thankful. Those mixed emotions made it easy to hold back but hard to keep them in. It was weird. But deep inside, those people were good people. They just thought differently.

So later on that day, I packed my bags and asked Carl if he could drop me off at the station. He accepted to take me. As we arrived at the station, I stretched out my hand. I thanked him and told him I wish everything would have worked out between us. He pulled my hand in and gave me a hug and accompanied it with an extra hundred dollars. He then apologized then thanked me. I could only wish his family blessings, and although things went a bit south, I was grateful for their sponsorship and the opportunity they gave me. The bus station lady called my number, and I hurried with my two luggages and my uncle Tonio's trash bag full of clothes. As I put the luggage away, the luggage boy asked if I could take the trash bag and put it up on the overhead storage room in the bus. I agreed and took it up with me. For a second or two, I was curious because the bag felt weird and was not that heavy. It was nothing but wrinkles. After all, it had been with me ever since we left El Paso, Texas. I was going take a look inside, but what was in there was none of my business. Plus it was my uncle's, so I left it at that.

On my trip back to my loved ones, I saw mountain after mountain, road after road, mile after mile, and desert after desert. We even hit a rough but beautiful dark thunderstorm through the mountains and deserts. I was sad but excited and could not wait to see my lovely wife, my kids, my parents, and my brother and sisters and their lovely kids. The roads were narrow, and the mountains were close to one another and super close to us. It seemed as if they were pushing us through. It was beautiful. I kind of felt like a cowboy who would be wanted dead or alive. The bus was our stagecoach, and my movie screen was the spectacular scenery. We made many, many stops from Amarillo, Texas, to Santa Rosa, New Mexico, and then to El Paso, Texas. I kind of got stop sick after a while. Regardless of my emotions, I had a deep wound. One of those that would not heal at the break of light. I was not going home the way I wanted to. I was not going home with enough money to do exactly what I wanted. My stomach would turn just as the thought would appear in my mind. I could not even eat. I felt an emptiness, and

I wondered, *Why do things like this keep happening to me this way? Why not the other way? You know, the good way. I believe in God. I have never killed anyone. I have never hurt nobody. Neither have I disrespected people. I work hard, and my mind is positive. Why is it that every time I am on a mission or say I am going to do something good, it does not happen? It's like the whole movement of the world is against me. Am I attracting this to my life, or are there stranger forces against me?* I was just trying to figure everything out when suddenly the bus driver announced our entrance to El Paso, Texas. As we were entering El Paso, I saw the night lights. They looked nice. They had a real big lit-up star on a big hill called the lone star that honorably respected the people of El Paso and their loved ones who were or had been in the service. It was a pretty cool view. And at that time, I was still wondering while looking at so many new model cars, so many stores packed with people, so many nice houses, *How? Why? I wish I could be in a good, wealthy, above average situation. I just want a future where I am not short of cash—with good health and a strong family.*

As we boarded off the bus and went into the bus station, an old man walked up to me and asked me where I was going. I told him I was going to the Juarez bus station in Mexico. He told me he was going to the same place I was going and offered to split a cab with me. I told him I was taking the bus. He replied by telling me there were no more buses at that hour until tomorrow, so I agreed to split the cab. As we went to the front of the bus station, we were waiting to wave down a cab. The man was telling me about his journey, which I did not care much to listen to. I just wanted to go home. I really don't remember all of what he said, but I remember two things he told me. And to this day, I still remember. He told me, "Look, muchacho (that means kid). Speak to your heart and listen to it when it answers back to you. This, your heart, knows more than you could ever imagine. And once you do, all your riches are just around the corner."

I responded stupidly, "Why do I want my riches around the corner?"

He replied, "Exactly! You want them with you." He laughed in a weird coughing, screeching way. His eerie laugh made me look at his face, because before that laugh, I was not paying that much attention to him. I saw his face, and it looked tired but alive. I then listened to what he was saying like if I was hypnotized by his voice of wisdom. He mentioned he needed to help a brother in need. This old man had thick silver-gray eyebrows. He sported long gray hair and a thin but long gray mustache. He looked, in a strange way, like a person from back in time. I mean, way back in time—kind of medieval or biblical times. He smelled like candy for some reason, gummy bear to be correct. He then replied, "Open your eyes and look deeper in your heart and you will see. Every dream can come true, but only you have to make it happen. And if you don't open your eyes, you might as well be blind."

I told him, "See what?"

He said, "Listen to me. Being blind with vision is like being alive but dead."

I told him, "Are you okay? Why are you talking like this? (He kind of gave me goosebumps.)

Chapter 9

Finally, there was a taxi in sight. I waved it down, and as soon as it stopped, I asked him, "How much to the Juarez bus station?" He said thirty dollars. I told him I would give him twenty. He agreed. So I asked him to pop the trunk, and as he did, I put my luggage in the trunk. The old man had a small leather bag he hand-carried. The old man did not say a word on our way to the bus station. As we were getting closer to the station, I started to feel sorry for the man. But my mind was off at that moment. I was thinking of home. I turned toward the old man, and he seemed very at peace with a high, strong voltage of energy coming out of that comforting everything-is-gonna-be-okay smile. I smiled back. The taxi driver was looking at me through his rearview mirror. He looked worried and puzzled at the same time. I ignored that look.

When we did finally get to the station, I walked out of the taxi. I lifted the trunk and grabbed my two luggages and my trash bag full of clothes. I left my bags on the sidewalk, went over to the driver, and asked him, "How much is it going to be for both of us?"

"Both of who?" the driver asked.

I looked around, and the old man was gone. I thought to myself, *The old man must have been in a hurry.* I mean, he disappeared quick—like magic. There was nobody in sight. The bus station was cold and silent outside. The taxi driver asked if I was on medication and said if I was, he wanted some. I asked, "What about the old man sitting next to me?"

The driver said, "There was nobody else in the taxi but you and me. Are you sure you're okay?" I felt freezing chills through my whole body.

I was speechless. The cab driver saw my pale face white as snow; I could tell he knew I was telling him the truth because he got pale himself. I looked at him, and he looked frightened. He said, "You don't have to pay me. I'm out of here!" He jumped in his taxi, and with a screech of the tires, he was gone. I didn't know what to think, and in a strange way, I thought to myself, *That old man was harmless.* Then I went into the stage of not accepting what I saw, which did not work as well as I thought. I closed my eyes and took a deep breath.

I was a bit shaken up, but then my family popped into my mind, and all of a sudden, it really didn't matter. Thinking of them comforts me. Being with them makes me happy and complete. So I picked up my bags and went inside the station to purchase my ticket. After my purchase, I had to pass my bags through inspection. It was pretty cool the way it worked. They had a small yellow street-like stoplight at the entrance. They had a green light that said "pass" and a red light that said "inspection." So if you'd press the button and the green light would flash, you'd walk through without being inspected. If the red light would flash, you'd go get your bags inspected and then pass. I had nothing to declare or hide but two luggages and a trash bag full of clothes. As I came up to the light, there was a small line of about eleven to twelve people. It took me about five minutes to reach the front. As I was getting ready to press the button, the taxi driver, who had dropped me off and did not charge me then took off with a frightened look on his face, was coming toward me. He yelled at me, saying, "Wait up! Don't leave! You left a bag in the car," catching the attention of the police and a few people who were present. He shouted again, "You left a bag behind! Here you go." I thought to myself, *Why would he even bother coming back after what had happened?* I thought maybe he was just an honest person. They do exist, you know. With no hesitation, he gave me the bag and said, "I want no problems."

I said, "Me neither." I looked at the bag and exclaimed to myself in a comforting way, *Aha! The old man's bag! I'm not that crazy after all. I knew it.* He handed me the bag, and before I had any time to thank him and tell him the bag was the old man's, he took off the same way he did on his taxicab. I got caught up in all the emotion when the guard told me not to waste his time and, in a good manner, told me to hurry up. I told the guard, "This is not my bag. I have to give it to the old man. It's his." I also had people in line behind me with an aggravated look on their faces. I looked around one last time, but no sign of the old man.

The guard told me, "It's in your hands. It's yours." Then he told me in a more forceful voice, "Now hurry before you get into problems." So I pressed the button. The green light lit up, and I was able to pass with no problems. I was a bit confused over the whole situation. I walked over to the luggage guy and gave him my luggage. He took my two luggage bags and my trash bag full of clothes then wrapped a blue paper ticket on a string to each of my items. He gave me the other half so I could identify them when we arrived at our destination. I took the old man's leather bag with me. I gave my ticket to the bus driver and boarded the bus. I finally sat down and laid my head back as I took a deep breath. I then got curious of what was in the bag. Maybe there was an address in there. So I opened it. It had a bunch of scrunched-up newspaper, like when you buy a new bag at the store. But this leather bag was old. I could not figure it out. All I could think about was him saying, "Look deeper inside your heart." And his expression as he was saying it crossed my mind.

I slept and awoke about half an hour before we got to the Chihuahua bus station. I then thought to myself, *I only have enough money for a couple of things—not for what I want to do. That means I have to get a job. I have to make something positive happen. I am grateful that I came back in one piece. I am grateful to God.* Then as we arrived at the bus station, with all the thoughts in my mind, I was pumped up and super happy to see my family. I picked up my luggage, and I almost ran out the station and boarded a taxicab in supersonic motion. I told the driver I was in a hurry and asked if he could keep that in consideration. We made it in a matter of no time. I paid the driver then took my stuff out the trunk and rushed for the door. It was past midnight when I knocked on the door. My father opened the door after about five minutes of knocking. He looked surprised. He shouted to my mom, "Hey, your son is here!" She came out all sleepy, rubbing her eyes. As she was on her way, my dad said in a sarcastic way, "You're back already! Did you go for vacation or what?"

I hugged him, kissed him, then told him, "Well, Dad, it was not a pleasant experience. And I did not make what I wanted to, but I have enough to be all right." My mother, on the other hand, was happy to see me as usual. My brother was sleeping, and I did not wake him. I was very happy to see my parents. I loved them so much. I asked for my wife and kids. They told me they were at my in-law's. My dad told me to wait till the next day, but I could not wait much longer. He could see it in my eyes.

Chapter 10

Believe me when I tell you that I felt energized when I saw them. I left my parents' house and went running to my mother-in-law's house. It was a good thing for me that it was only about five blocks away. I knocked on her door and was lucky enough for her to answer the door. My wife looked so beautiful. I hugged her and kissed her, and all the hurt I felt inside was gone and emptied out with each second of hugging her. The hurt was no longer there. I felt my emptiness fill up with love. I did not want to let her go, but I also wanted to see my wonderful kids. They were all sleeping. I did not wake them. I simply kissed them many, many times until they woke up. They looked at me and smiled. I loved them so much.

The next morning, we all got up and went home. As soon as we got there, I asked my mom if she had my uncle Tonio's phone number so I could call him and return his bag. My mom replied, "You mean to tell me you carried that bag all the time you were gone?"

I told her, "Yes, I did."

She said, "How inconsiderate of him."

I told her, "No, it's okay. He was going to catch up to me in Denver, but I guess he didn't. And it's a good thing he didn't." Then she gave me his number. After I made that call, my life totally changed. After that, I have been able to see things in a more miraculous way than ever. I picked up the phone and dialed the number. He answered the phone. I said, "Hey, what's up, Tio (that means *uncle* in Spanish)?"

He recognized my voice and said, "Hey, where are you?"

I told him, "Here at home."

He asked, "What happened? Weren't you supposed to come after the snow season?" I told him it did not go as good as I thought it would so I came back. He said, "It's a good thing I didn't go."

I told him, "Yeah, you lucked out. It was rough." Then I asked him, "By the way, Tonio, I have your bag. Can you come pick it up, or do you want me to drop it off at your house?"

He said, "What bag?"

I told him, "The bag you told me to take with me then when you caught up with me you would take it back."

"No, no, no, when we said goodbye, I changed my mind and went back and asked Pepe for my bags. He gave them to me. I then asked for you, but he said you went to the restroom. So I hurried back to catch my bus back home."

"How come you didn't wait for me?" I responded.

He said, "I don't know."

I told him, "Are you sure it's not yours?"

He responded, "Yes, I am. Why wouldn't I be sure? You sound weird. Are you okay?"

I told him, "Yeah, I'm fine. Well, I'll see you later." And I hung up. I thought to myself, *It could not have been Pepe's or his aunt's. How did that get in there? We were at the border when we put our luggage back in the trunk. Pepe had one bag. His aunt also had one bag. Tonio had two, and I had two. But then again, I didn't see him take his bags.* A voice out of nowhere popped into my mind. It said, "Look deeper into your heart. Look harder. It's just around the corner." I snapped out of it and thought to myself, *It has to belong to someone.* Just then, my wife walked in the kitchen, where I was at that moment, and asked me, "Are you all right?" I looked at her and told her what was happening with this mysterious trash bag full of clothes. She thought I was going crazy. Then she said, "Why don't you open it? It might have information on whom it belongs to."

I told her, "You're right. Come on. Let's go and open it." The bag was in my room, and we rushed to it. As we went in the room, I picked the bag up and said, "Here we go" as if I was bungee jumping off the highest cliff in the world. And I did feel my stomach turn as I was opening it. I opened it, and it was full of insulation cloth. I opened the cloth, and to my amazement, I almost fainted. Heck, my wife almost fainted too. As I began to open it, I saw some cash. And the more I opened it, the more cash there was. The bag was full of cash. I was at a lost for words. "Can you just imagine that? I went all over the central part of the United States with frostbite, failure after failure, taking abuse, being hungry, being criticized, ridiculed, and laughed at and I had a bag full of cash with me all the time." I said all this in a loud outspoken way. My mother, father, brother, and kids rushed in the room. My dad asked, "What's going on?"

Then my wife asked me, "Is that yours?"

I told her, "No, it's not. Now what?" My whole family was looking at me as if I had robbed a bank or something. I did not complain or say anything. I opened the whole bag. We counted the money. Fifty thousand dollars—wow! As I got to the bottom of the bag, there was a picture of Saint Jude with a handwritten scroll on the back. I remembered—I had been upset at Saint Jude for many years, and more eerie than that, the man who smelled of gummy bear candy looked exactly like Saint Jude's picture. It blew my mind away. I thought to myself, *Could it have been him?* I took a deep breath, which I was getting used to doing. I shook my head and closed my eyes. When I opened them, I saw another piece of paper that read, "The beginning of a good start." I looked at my family, and they were all looking at me. My dad said, "Read it." While I had a confused look, they looked excited. I was just trying to piece everything together. I felt a tingling sensation all over my body; I felt blessed. As I read the letter out loud, my family and I burst into tears with joy.

Letter

You don't have to believe in me if you don't want to, but just believe. Open your eyes and look deeper into your heart and listen to it. You see, my journey was to help you in a magical way. I put the bag of money in front of your eyes on your road of life. You were not able to see it until you were ready. I followed you from the US border to Phoenix to Denver to Breckenridge and back to Denver. From Denver to Dalhart to New Mexico. And your journey from El Paso to Juarez. You're a funny guy, hardheaded but a sweet, funny guy. I like you, and that is why I had to go in that cab and drop the letter at the bottom of the bag. It was a journey in itself. My old leather bag is full of wrinkled-up paper. That bag is as old as the city you live in—maybe older. Please do me a favor. Empty out the old leather bag. Fill it with as much cash as you can from the trash bag full of money. Donate it to a needy cause. I know you will pick the right one. Keep the rest of the money for yourself, and enjoy your dreams and the rest of your special journey. God bless you and our family.

PS I am future you. And I just want to let you know everything works out (just believe).
Then all I've said
heard, and done,
it popped in my heart.
I never thought of faith,
and well, you got to have
faith.
Toto

Lightning Source UK Ltd.
Milton Keynes UK
UKHW011853301120
374378UK00012B/1379/J